ZEBRAS

AFRICAN ANIMAL DISCOVERY LIBRARY

Lynn M. Stone

Rourke Corporation, Inc.
Vero Beach, Florida 32964

PHOTO CREDITS

All photos by the Author

LIBRARY OF CONGRESS
Library of Congress Cataloging-in-Publication Data
Stone, Lynn M.
  Zebras / by Lynn M. Stone.

    p. cm. — (African animal discovery library)
    Summary: Describes the physical characteristics, habitat,
and behavior of the zebra.
    ISBN 0-86593-048-1
    1. Zebras—Juvenile literature. [1. Zebras.] I. Title.
II. Series: Stone, Lynn M. African animal discovery library.
QL737.U62S76   1990
599.72'5—dc20   89-48441
                                   CIP
                                   AC

Burchell's zebra drinking

TABLE OF CONTENTS

THE ZEBRA

Zebras are Africa's "painted" ponies. They are wild horses with stripes.

Each zebra looks like it was painted by hand. No zebra has stripes just like another's.

Like horses, zebras are **grazers.** They chew grass as they move across African **savannas.** Savannas are the wide, grassy lands where many zebras live.

Three kinds, or **species,** of zebras live in Africa. The most common of them is Burchell's zebra *(Hippotigris quagga).* The others are Grevy's zebra *(Hippotigris grevyi)* and the mountain zebra *(Hippotigris zebra).*

THE ZEBRA'S COUSINS

The zebra's closest cousins are horses, both wild and **domestic.** Domestic horses are raised for farming and riding.

True wild horses, other than zebras, are found in Asia and Africa. The "wild" horses of the American West are domestic horses living in the wild.

One true wild horse, the Przewalski's horse of Asia, looks very much like a small domestic horse. The African wild ass is another of the zebra's wild relatives. It looks like a donkey or burro.

Domestic pony

HOW THEY LOOK

Like a horse, a zebra has a rounded body, slim legs, and a ridge of hair along its neck. That is the zebra's mane. The zebra's black stripes and thin tail make it easy to tell from a horse.

The three species of zebras can usually be told apart by their size and the location of their stripes. The Grevy's zebra, for example, has more narrow stripes than other zebras.

A Grevy's zebra male, or stallion, may weigh nearly 950 pounds. Burchell's zebras weigh up to 780 pounds. Mountain zebras weigh up to 660 pounds.

Zebras are not as large as big horses.

Zebra drinking

WHERE THEY LIVE

Zebras are found in many places in Africa, which is their only home.

Burchell's zebra, sometimes called the "common" zebra, lives in eastern and southeastern Africa. Grevy's zebra lives in eastern Africa. The mountain zebra lives in southern Africa.

Zebras like open country with plenty of grass and not too many trees. Open ground allows them to look for enemies and run from them.

Some zebra herds travel many miles to find greener pastures.

Zebra herd

Zebra and antelope

HOW THEY LIVE

Zebras are alert, active animals. They spend much of the day and part of the night feeding. They also find time to rest, drink, and take dust baths in the dirt.

Zebras are usually found in herds. A herd may be made up of several zebra families or of groups of stallions.

A zebra family has one stallion with several females (mares) and their babies, called **foals.** Stallions often fight for the mares. They wrestle with their necks and kick with their front feet.

Zebras have good vision and hearing. Their "talk" back and forth includes snorts, squeals, and whinnies.

Zebra in dust wallow

THE ZEBRA'S BABIES

A zebra mare usually gives birth to just one foal. The foal lives on its mother's milk for the first few days of life. Then it begins nibbling at grass too.

At about one year of age, young zebras leave their mothers. Mares usually join with a stallion. Young male zebras live together in groups of two to 10.

Captive zebras have reached 40 years. Wild zebras probably live until they are about 20.

Zebra mare and foal

PREDATOR AND PREY

Zebras live by eating plants, mostly grass. Zebras have nothing to fear from other animals that live on plants. Large, plant-eating animals such as antelope and giraffes often feed with zebras.

Large, meat-eating animals called **predators,** however, are a constant danger to zebras. The most dangerous predator is the lion.

Zebras are also **prey,** or food, for African hunting dogs, spotted hyenas, leopards, and cheetahs. These predators usually attack zebra foals.

Lions at zebra kill

ZEBRAS AND PEOPLE

The **population,** or total number, of zebras has become smaller in recent years. Zebras have been killed for their skins and because they eat grass.

Ranchers don't like to share grass with zebras. They like to keep the wild grass for their sheep and cattle.

Another problem for zebras is less grass. As more farm animals are raised in Africa, they eat more grass.

In southern Africa, settlers from Europe made one kind of zebra, the quagga, **extinct**—gone forever. The last quagga died in 1883.

The quagga had fewer stripes than other zebras. Some had almost no stripes at all.

Endangered Grevy's zebra

THE ZEBRA'S FUTURE

With one kind of zebra already extinct, what is the future of the others?

Grevy's zebra is on the **endangered** species list in some parts of East Africa. Endangered animals are in danger of becoming extinct.

Mountain zebras are also endangered. Thirty years ago there were 100,000. Now there may be 2,000 mountain zebras.

Burchell's zebras are the most common zebras. But as Africa's human population grows, even these zebras may someday be found only in wildlife parks.

Glossary

domestic (dum ES tik)—tamed and raised by man

endangered (en DANE jerd)—in danger of no longer existing; very rare

extinct (ex TINKT)—the point at which an animal species no longer exists, such as the quagga

foal (FOAL)—a baby zebra or horse

grazer (GRAY zer)—an animal which feeds on grass or other low plants of the field

population (pop u LAY shun)—all the animals of one species, such as the total number of Burchell's zebras

predator (PRED a tor)—an animal that kills other animals for food

prey (PREY)—an animal that is hunted by another for food

savanna (sa VAN nuh)—broad, grassy areas with few trees

species (SPEE sheez)—within a group of closely related animals, one certain kind

INDEX

4843